JOSEPH MIDTHUN   SAMUEL HITI

BUILDING BLOCKS OF SCIENCE

MATTER

and its properties

WORLD
BOOK

a Scott Fetzer company
Chicago

www.worldbookonline.com

World Book, Inc.
233 N. Michigan Avenue
Chicago, IL 60601
U.S.A.

For information about other World Book publications, visit our website at http://www.worldbookonline.com or call 1-800-WORLDBK (967-5325).

For information about sales to schools and libraries, call 1-800-975-3250 (United States); 1-800-837-5365 (Canada).

ATTENTION, READER!

Some characters in this series throw large objects from tall buildings, play with fire, ride on bicycle handlebars, and perform other dangerous acts. However, they are CARTOON CHARACTERS. Please do not try any of these things at home because you could seriously harm yourself—or others around you!

Library of Congress Cataloging-in-Publication Data

Matter and its properties.
    p. cm. -- (Building blocks of science)
  Includes index.
  Summary: "A graphic nonfiction volume that introduces the properties of matter. Features include several photographic pages, a glossary, additional resource list, and an index"--Provided by publisher.
  ISBN 978-0-7166-1429-6
  1. Matter--Properties--Juvenile literature. I. World Book, Inc.
QC173.16.M38 2012
530--dc23
                                2011025905

Building Blocks of Science
Set ISBN: 978-0-7166-1420-3

Printed in China by Leo Paper Products LTD., Heshan, Guangdong
1st printing December 2011

Acknowledgments:
Created by Samuel Hiti and Joseph Midthun.
Art by Samuel Hiti. Written by Joseph Midthun.

© Dreamstime 8; © istockphoto 11; © Shutterstock 8, 9, 10; © FoodCollection/SuperStock 11; WORLD BOOK illustration by Linda Kinnaman 24-25.

STAFF
Executive Committee
President: Donald D. Keller
Vice President and Editor in Chief: Paul A. Kobasa
Vice President, Marketing/
  Digital Products: Sean Klunder
Vice President, International: Richard Flower
Director, Human Resources: Bev Ecker

Editorial
Associate Manager, Supplementary
  Publications: Cassie Mayer
Writer and Letterer: Joseph Midthun
Editors: Mike DuRoss and Brian Johnson
Researcher: Annie Brodsky
Manager, Contracts & Compliance
  (Rights & Permissions): Loranne K. Shields

Manufacturing/Pre-Press/Graphics and Design
Director: Carma Fazio
Manufacturing Manager: Steven Hueppchen
Production/Technology Manager:
  Anne Fritzinger
Proofreader: Emilie Schrage
Manager, Graphics and Design: Tom Evans
Coordinator, Design Development and
  Production: Brenda B. Tropinski
Book Design: Samuel Hiti
Photographs Editor: Kathy Creech

TABLE OF CONTENTS

There is a glossary on page 30. Terms defined in the glossary are in type **that looks like this** on their first appearance.

The ground under your feet is made of matter.

The water in a river is made of matter.

The clouds above you are made of matter.

The stars in the sky are made of matter.

Even *you* are made of matter.

Matter is anything that has **mass** and **volume**.

PROPERTIES OF MATTER

Mass, volume, and density are **properties** of matter.

Properties of matter can be used to describe objects.

COLOR

TEXTURE

SHAPE

SIZE

These pages show examples of some properties of matter you can see or feel.

Some properties of matter are invisible.

But you can test matter to find them.

For example, you can test matter to see...

...whether it floats or sinks.

...if it is **attracted** to magnets.

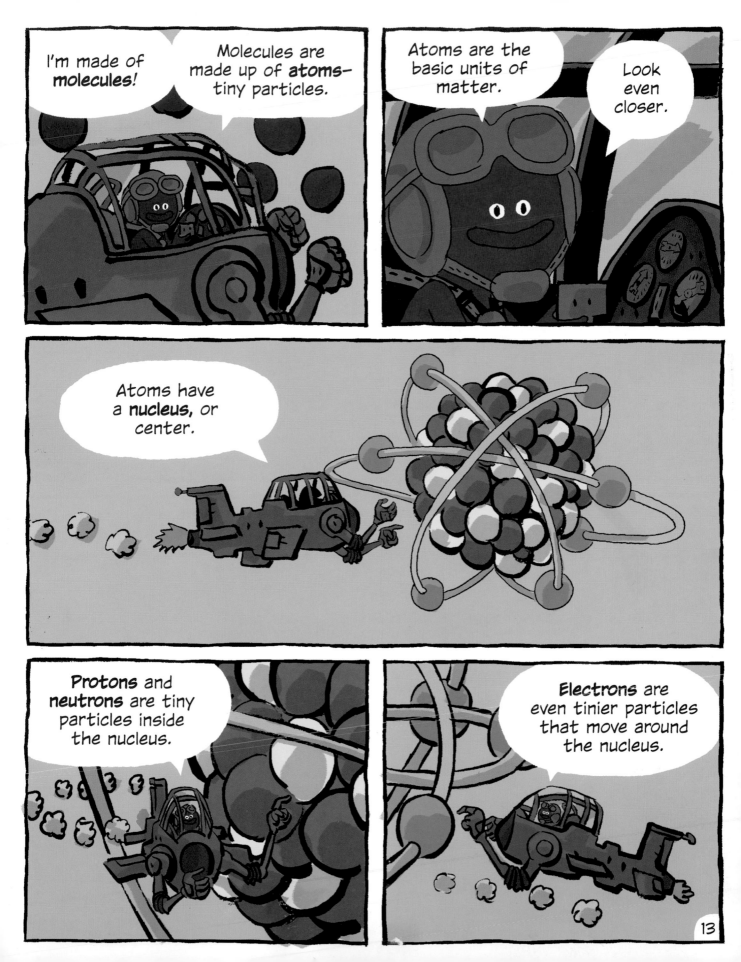

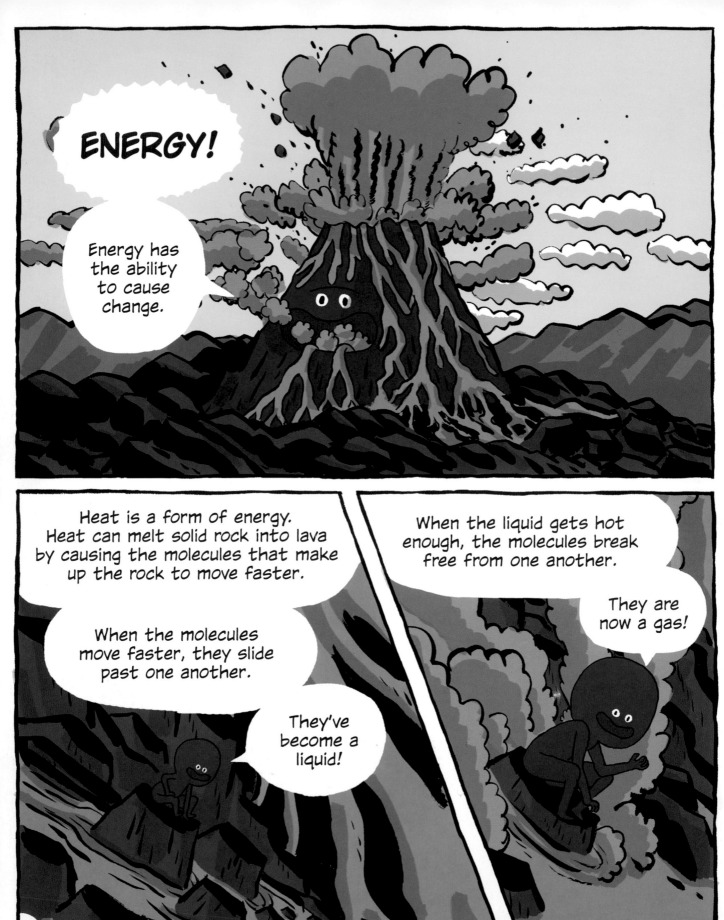

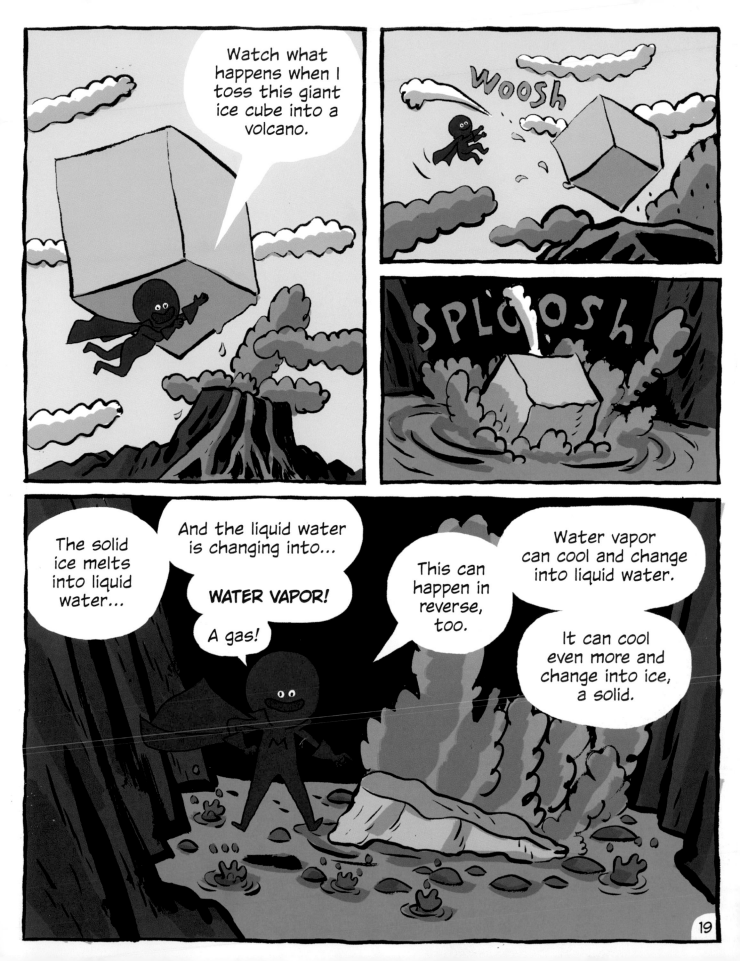

Nonmetals are a much smaller group of elements than metals.
But nonmetals can be quite different from one another.
Nearly all metals are solid at room temperature. But nonmetals can be solids, liquids, or gases.
The carbon in bones is a solid nonmetal.
And the oxygen you breathe is a nonmetal gas.

THE PERIODIC TABLE

The **periodic table** lists all the elements that scientists have identified so far.

Metals are on one side of the table and nonmetals, except hydrogen, are on the other side.

Each element has its own symbol. Remember when we made a molecule of water?

I called it H_2O.

Here's why!

You can read the table like this...

	1										
		2	3	4	5	6	7	8	9		
1	1 **H** Hydrogen										
2	3 **Li** Lithium	4 **Be** Beryllium									
3	11 **Na** Sodium	12 **Mg** Magnesium									
4	19 **K** Potassium	20 **Ca** Calcium	21 **Sc** Scandium	22 **Ti** Titanium	23 **V** Vanadium	24 **Cr** Chromium	25 **Mn** Manganese	26 **Fe** Iron	27 **Co** Cobalt		
5	37 **Rb** Rubidium	38 **Sr** Strontium	39 **Y** Yttrium	40 **Zr** Zirconium	41 **Nb** Niobium	42 **Mo** Molybdenum	43 **Tc** Technetium	44 **Ru** Ruthenium	45 **Rh** Rhodium		
6	55 **Cs** Cesium	56 **Ba** Barium		72 **Hf** Hafnium	73 **Ta** Tantalum	74 **W** Tungsten	75 **Re** Rhenium	76 **Os** Osmium	77 **Ir** Iridium		
7	87 **Fr** Francium	88 **Ra** Radium		104 **Rf** Rutherfordium	105 **Db** Dubnium	106 **Sg** Seaborgium	107 **Bh** Bohrium	108 **Hs** Hassium	109 **Mt** Meitnerium		

57 **La** Lanthanum	58 **Ce** Cerium	59 **Pr** Praseodymium	60 **Nd** Neodymium	61 **Pm** Promethium	62 **Sm** Samarium	63 **Eu** Europium
89 **Ac** Actinium	90 **Th** Thorium	91 **Pa** Protactinium	92 **U** Uranium	93 **Np** Neptunium	94 **Pu** Plutonium	95 **Am** Americium

Atomic Number
Atomic Symbol
Atomic Name

1 **H** Hydrogen

The symbol for hydrogen is *H*— get it?

"H" for hydrogen.

"O" for oxygen.

So the symbol for a molecule of water, two hydrogen atoms and one oxygen atom, is H_2O!

			13	14	15	16	17	18
								2 **He** Helium
			5 **B** Boron	6 **C** Carbon	7 **N** Nitrogen	8 **O** Oxygen	9 **F** Fluorine	10 **Ne** Neon
10	11	12	13 **Al** Aluminum	14 **Si** Silicon	15 **P** Phosphorus	16 **S** Sulfur	17 **Cl** Chlorine	18 **Ar** Argon
28 **Ni** Nickel	29 **Cu** Copper	30 **Zn** Zinc	31 **Ga** Gallium	32 **Ge** Germanium	33 **As** Arsenic	34 **Se** Selenium	35 **Br** Bromine	36 **Kr** Krypton
46 **Pd** Palladium	47 **Ag** Silver	48 **Cd** Cadmium	49 **In** Indium	50 **Sn** Tin	51 **Sb** Antimony	52 **Te** Tellurium	53 **I** Iodine	54 **Xe** Xenon
78 **Pt** Platinum	79 **Au** Gold	80 **Hg** Mercury	81 **Tl** Thallium	82 **Pb** Lead	83 **Bi** Bismuth	84 **Po** Polonium	85 **At** Astatine	86 **Rn** Radon
110 **Ds** Darmstadtium	111 **Rg** Roentgenium	112 **Cn** Copernicium	113 * Unutrium	114 * Flerovium	115 * Ununpentium	116 * Moscovium	117 * Ununseptium	118 * Ununoctium

64 **Gd** Gadolinium	65 **Tb** Terbium	66 **Dy** Dysprosium	67 **Ho** Holmium	68 **Er** Erbium	69 **Tm** Thulium	70 **Yb** Ytterbium	71 **Lu** Lutetium
96 **Cm** Curium	97 **Bk** Berkelium	98 **Cf** Californium	99 **Es** Einsteinium	100 **Fm** Fermium	101 **Md** Mendelevium	102 **No** Nobelium	103 **Lr** Lawrencium

*Atomic symbol to be determined

Metals	Metalloids	Nonmetals

GLOSSARY

atom one of the basic units of matter.

attract to pull one object toward another.

compound a substance that contains more than one kind of atom.

conductor something that allows heat, electricity, light, sound, or other form of energy to pass through it.

contract to decrease in size.

density the amount of matter in a particular volume of a substance.

electron a kind of particle that circles around the nucleus (center) of an atom. Electrons have a negative electric charge.

element a substance made of only one kind of atom.

expand to increase in size.

mass the amount of matter in an object.

matter what all things are made of.

metal any of a large group of elements that includes copper, gold, iron, lead, silver, tin, and other elements that share similar qualities.

molecule Two or more atoms chemically bonded together.

neutron a kind of particle inside the nucleus (center) of an atom. Neutrons have no electric charge.

nonmetal materials that do not have the properties of metals. Wood, glass, plastic, and rock are examples of nonmetals.

nucleus the center of an atom. Protons and neutrons are inside the nucleus.

periodic table a chart that lists the known chemical elements arranged according to their characteristics.

property quality or power belonging specially to something.

proton a kind of particle inside the nucleus (center) of an atom. Neutrons have a positive electric charge.

states of matter the different forms of matter. The most familiar are solid, liquid, and gas.

volume the amount of space something takes up.

water vapor water in the state of a gas.

FIND OUT MORE

Books

Change It! Solids, Liquids, Gases and You by Adrienne Mason and Claudia Davila (Kids Can Press, 2006)

Matter by Christopher Cooper (DK Publishing, 1999)

Mixtures and Compounds by Alastair Smith, Philip Clarke, and Corinne Henderson (Usborne, 2002)

Physics: Why Matter Matters! by Dan Green and Simon Basher (Kingfisher, 2008)

Science Fair Projects About the Properties of Matter: Using Marbles, Water, Balloons, and More by Robert Gardner (Enslow Publishers, 2004)

Science Measurements: How Heavy? How Long? How Hot? By Chris Eboch and Jon Davis (Picture Window Books, 2007)

Touch It! Materials, Matter, and You by Adrienne Mason and Claudia Davila (Kids Can Press, 2005)

What Is Matter? by Don L. Curry (Children's Press, 2004)

Websites

The Atom Builder
http://www.pbs.org/wgbh/aso/tryit/atom/
The tiny, mighty atom is made up of even smaller parts! Build your own atoms at this website from PBS's A Science Odyssey.

The Atoms Family
http://www.miamisci.org/af/sln/
Learn about the basic building blocks of matter—atoms—at this educational site from the Science Learning Network.

Chem4Kids: States of Matter
http://www.chem4kids.com/files/matter_states.html
Learn more about the states of matter at this fun and educational chemistry site.

Little Shop of Physics
http://littleshop.physics.colostate.edu/amazingphysics.htm
At this website, you will find experiments in force, energy, and motion, along with other basic physics concepts.

Marvelous Molecules
http://www.nyhallsci.org/marvelousmolecules/
Check out this website for activities and information about the molecules that make up the world around us.

The Particle Adventure
http://particleadventure.org/
Explore the fundamentals of matter and force at this educational website from the Particle Data Group.

Strange Matter
http://www.StrangeMatterExhibit.com/
What makes up all the things around us? What makes different materials so different? Find out more about matter and materials at this website.

INDEX